# The Fuel
## of the Future

by Vanessa York

# Introduction

Fuel is any material that stores energy that can be **extracted** and then used. Wood was probably the first fuel that people used. The energy of the wood was extracted by fire.

Today, we use fuel to run vehicles, machines, and appliances. We also use it to make electricity.

We need fuel to help us get around.

Many trucks run on diesel fuel, which is made from oil.

People have been using **fossil fuels**, such as coal, natural gas, and oil, for hundreds of years. These are fuels that we find in the earth, but there are some big problems with them. Fossil fuels cause pollution. They also produce **greenhouse gases**, such as carbon dioxide. Greenhouse gases act like the roof of a greenhouse, trapping heat in Earth's atmosphere. Some scientists think that the increase in greenhouse gases may be causing **global warming** and climate change. Fossil fuels are also running out.

What are the alternatives? Scientists are working hard to come up with some answers.

# CHAPTER 1

# Biofuels

Biofuel is a type of fuel that is made from renewable resources, such as soy bean plants. Biofuel can also be made from treated natural waste products, such as animal fats and used vegetable oil. It produces far less pollution than traditional fuels. There is a lot of interest in biofuels today.

## Plant Sugars and Ethanol

Plants are full of sugar. This sugar can be used to make the biofuel ethanol. To make ethanol, plants are ground up and mixed with water and enzymes. Yeast is added to the mixture. The plant sugars ferment, turning into ethanol. Ethanol can be used in gas engines as a replacement for gasoline.

Corn is turned into ethanol at this plant in Iowa.

Henry Ford's Model T was first designed to run on ethanol.

Biofuel is not a new idea. Rudolf Diesel invented the diesel engine. He knew that his engine would run on vegetable oil. In 1900, Diesel demonstrated it running on peanut oil. Henry Ford also expected his Model T car to run on ethanol produced from corn. Then gasoline became cheap and easily available. Cars fueled by gasoline became popular, so biofuels did not become widely used. Today, people are turning to biofuels again out of concern for the environment.

Some public transportation is run on biofuel, helping to cut city pollution.

Ethanol is the most commonly used biofuel. It is made from plants such as wheat, potatoes, corn, and sugar beet. Bioethanol can also be made from seaweed algae.

Ethanol is mostly used to run cars. It is mixed with gasoline to make a fuel that is cleaner than plain gasoline. In Brazil, a country that has a thriving biofuel industry, about 20% of all cars run on ethanol.

## Ethanol Fuel Production in 2010

| | |
|---|---|
| United States | 13,230 million gallons |
| Brazil | 6,922 million gallons |
| European Union | 1,177 million gallons |
| China | 542 million gallons |
| Canada | 357 million gallons |

Not everyone thinks biofuel is good for the environment. Bioethanol does not pollute the environment as much as gasoline. However, that's only part of the story. It takes seven acres of corn to produce enough bioethanol to run one car for one year. That's a lot of land that could also be used to produce food.

In some places, such as Indonesia, rain forest has been cut down to make way for biofuel crops. This loss of habitat has had a devastating effect on many endangered animals.

It may be possible to grow seaweed in the ocean in large quantities for ethanol. Scientists are working on this idea.

A large amount of the corn grown in the United States is used to make ethanol.

Grown for Biofuel

This scientist is researching plant bacteria that may be useful in making biofuel.

Biobutanol is made from plant material in a similar way to ethanol. Scientists are excited by the potential of this biofuel. Their research has found that biobutanol can be made by bacteria such as *e.coli. E.coli* is a bacteria that causes upset stomachs!

Right now, biobutanol is very expensive to produce. Scientists hope that they will be able to improve the process and make it a renewable fuel that may help replace fossil fuels.

Biodiesel is the most common biofuel in Europe. Biodiesel is made from oils or fats, such as soy, palm oil, and algae. Scientists have even managed to make biodiesel from used coffee grounds!

Biodiesel looks a lot like ordinary diesel. Diesel is a fuel made from oil. Unlike ordinary diesel, biodiesel is **non-toxic** and **biodegradable**. It can also be used in just about any diesel engine. Often biodiesel is mixed with ordinary diesel fuel.

Diesel is used to run heavy machinery as well as many cars and trucks.

Biodiesel is available in many places, where people can buy it at a gas station. There are some problems with biodiesel, however. It causes less pollution than ordinary diesel, but it still produces fumes that cause smog. Biodiesel is also expensive to make. Scientists are looking at ways to improve this fuel.

## *Earthrace*

# *Around the World*

In 2008, *Earthrace*, a cool-looking powerboat that ran entirely on biodiesel, broke the world speed record for circumnavigating the globe. The boat made the trip in 60 days, 23 hours, and 49 minutes.

# CHAPTER 2

# Hydrogen Fuel

Imagine a car that runs on water! Maybe in the future, cars will. Hydrogen is a colorless, odorless gas. When hydrogen is burned as a fuel, it produces almost no pollution at all. It is also very powerful. NASA uses hydrogen fuel to launch rockets and spacecraft into orbit.

Hydrogen is not often found by itself. It is usually found in water in combination with oxygen. It is also found in **hydrocarbons**. Hydrocarbons are in many fuels, such as gasoline and natural gas.

NASA uses hydrogen fuel to launch rockets and other spacecraft into orbit.

Making hydrogen fuel involves separating the hydrogen from the oxygen in water. This can be done with an electrical current. Hydrogen fuel can also be made by separating it from hydrocarbons using heat.

However it is done, separating hydrogen takes a lot of energy. It also costs a lot of money. Scientists hope that their research will eventually make hydrogen fuel widely available.

## Hydrogen Power

The first hydrogen power plant opened in Italy in 2009. The plant is supplying power to 20,000 homes. It prevents thousands of tons of greenhouse gases every year.

Hydrogen power helps provide electricity to the city of Venice, Italy.

Today, hydrogen fuel is mostly used in fuel cells. Fuel cells combine hydrogen and oxygen, which causes a chemical reaction. Fuel cells convert the energy of this chemical reaction to electricity. Fuel cells also release water, but the water is so clean that astronauts in space drink it!

Hydrogen fuel has a lot of potential as a fuel of the future. Unlike biofuels, it causes almost no pollution. Scientists are working on ways to use hydrogen fuel to run cars and airplanes.

## A Hydrogen Fuel Cell

Hydrogen and oxygen are combined in a fuel cell. Electricity is generated. Water is also released.

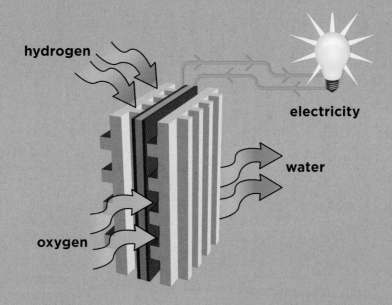

hydrogen

electricity

water

oxygen

# Conclusion

The fuels of the future must be renewable. Scientists are working hard to discover new ways to do things. They are working to make processes more efficient. Their work will result in fuels that cost less to produce. That will mean they are cheaper for people to use.

The fuels of the future must also come from sources that are sustainable. Here, too, scientists are working to discover and improve new technologies. We must make wise use of Earth's resources, because not all of them are renewable.

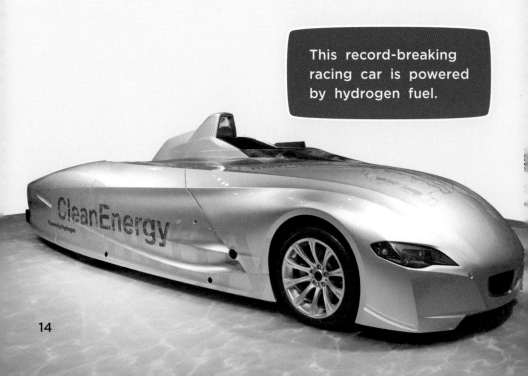

This record-breaking racing car is powered by hydrogen fuel.

# Respond to Reading

## Summarize

Use details from the text to summarize what you have learned about fuels of the future.

| Cause | → | Effect |
|---|---|---|
| First | → | |
| Next | → | |
| Then | → | |
| Finally | → | |

## Text Evidence

1. *The Fuel of the Future* is an expository text. This type of text gives information about a topic. Find two pieces of information about biofuels in the text. **GENRE**

2. How does using fossil fuels affect the environment? **CAUSE AND EFFECT**

3. Homophones are words that sound the same but have different meanings. Find the homophones on page 5. **HOMOPHONES**

4. Use details from the text to summarize what you have learned about fuels of the future. Use details from the text to support your answer. **WRITE ABOUT READING**

**Compare Texts**
Read about ways you and your family can
save energy.

# Saving Energy

We depend on energy in our homes. We need
it to heat our homes in winter and cool them
during the summer. It takes energy to heat the
water we use to take showers, as well as the
water we use to wash our dishes and clothes.
It also takes energy to run our televisions,
computers, and appliances.

There are, however, many simple ways we can
save energy. Using less energy means that we
save money and help the planet, too.

Keeping doors, curtains, and blinds closed when
it is cold will save energy in heating. Keeping
doors and windows open in warmer weather helps
cool the air without using any energy. When it is
very hot out, keep the curtains closed for shade
during the day.

Turn off the tap while you are brushing your teeth. That will not only save water; it will save energy, too. The greatest use of electricity in most cities comes from supplying water and taking away wastewater.

It's not just taps that should be turned off whenever possible. Light switches should, too. If you are leaving a room, turn off the lights. Appliances such as televisions should also be turned off at the wall when they are not in use. They can drain power even if they are switched off. Switch to energy-saving lightbulbs to save even more.

 If you leave a room, switch off the light behind you.

# TOP TIPS TO SAVE ENERGY

1. **Turn it off!** That means the light switch, the television, the stereo—if you've finished with it, switch it off.

2. **Keep it closed!** The refrigerator and the oven both work much more efficiently when the door is closed. Closing doors inside the house helps keep heat in.

3. **Look for the label!** Appliances such as washing machines, refrigerators, and dryers that are energy efficient have a special "energy star" label. Energy-efficient lightbulbs also help save energy.

 An energy-efficient lightbulb uses 75% less energy.

 **Make Connections**
What do you think is the main idea of *Saving Energy*? ESSENTIAL QUESTION

What theme does *The Fuel of the Future* share with *Saving Energy*? TEXT TO TEXT

# Glossary

**biodegradable** *(BIGH-oh-di-GRAY-duh-buhl)* able to decompose, or break down, naturally *(page 9)*

**extracted** *(eks-TRAKT-uhd)* taken out of something or from somewhere *(page 2)*

**fossil fuels** *(FOS-uhl FEW-uhlz)* fuels that are formed from the remains of ancient plants and animals, such as oil and natural gas *(page 3)*

**global warming** *(GLOH-buhl WAWRM-ing)* the increase in Earth's surface temperature due to the greenhouse effect *(page 3)*

**greenhouse gases** *(GREEN-hows GAS-uhz)* gases, such as carbon dioxide, that get trapped in Earth's atmosphere, making it hotter *(page 3)*

**hydrocarbons** *(HIGH-droh-KAHR-buhnz)* organic compounds of hydrogen and carbon, found in crude oil *(page 11)*

**non-toxic** *(non-TOK-sik)* safe, harmless to the environment *(page 9)*

# Index

**Purpose** To find out how a gas (carbon dioxide) rises from liquid

## What You Need

- a bottle of soda
- a balloon
- a watch or clock

## What To Do

**Step 1** Open a bottle of soda.

**Step 2** Put the end of the balloon over the neck of the bottle. Make sure it fits tightly.

**Step 3** Check the balloon every ten minutes for changes.

**Step 4** Record what you see.

**Conclusion** What happened to the balloon?